DECADES OF THE
20TH
CENTURY

1920s

ELDORADO INK

DECADES OF THE 20TH CENTURY

1900s

1910s

1920s

1930s

1940s

1950s

1960s

1970s

1980s

1990s

DECADES OF THE
20TH CENTURY

1920s

ELDORADO INK

Published by Eldorado Ink
2099 Lost Oak Trail
Prescott, AZ 86303
www.eldoradoink.com

Milan Bobek, Editor
Judith C. Callomon, Historical consultant
Samuel J. Patti, Consulting editor

Printed and bound in Slovenia

Publisher Cataloging Data
1920s / [Milan Bobek, editor].
        p. cm. -- (Decades of the 20th century)
        Includes index.
        Summary: This volume, arranged chronologically, presents
key events that have shaped the decade, from significant political
occurrences to details of daily life.
        ISBN 1-932904-02-6
        1. Nineteen twenties   2. History, Modern--20th century--
Chronology   3. History, Modern--20th century--Pictorial works
I. Bobek, Milan   II. Title: Nineteen twenties   III. Series
        909.82/2--dc22

Picture research and photography by Anne Hobart Lang and Rolf
Lang of AHL Archives. Additional research by Heritage Picture
Collection, London.

CONTENTS

THE JAZZ AGE

The decade of the 1920s reaps the whirlwind of World War I. People seem determined to live faster and more furiously. Fashions, hair, music, and the arts become thoroughly modern, with the change particularly affecting women. Travel becomes easier as ships and airplanes make the globe a smaller place. The economic consequences of war are felt at the end of the decade when financial depression, originated on Wall Street, sweeps across the States and then the rest of the world, making the ground fertile for unrest and further conflict.

OPPOSITE: The Wall Street Crash triggers panic and global economic depression.

1920–1929

KEY EVENTS OF THE DECADE

- PROHIBITION IN UNITED STATES
- CHINESE COMMUNIST PARTY ESTABLISHED
- IRISH FREE STATE ESTABLISHED
- MUSSOLINI SEIZES POWER
- RUSSIA BECOMES THE U.S.S.R.
- FIRST NAZI RALLY IN GERMANY
- SURREALIST MANIFESTO PUBLISHED
- STALIN RISES TO POWER
- SCOPES TRIAL IN UNITED STATES

- SAUDI ARABIA ESTABLISHED
- BAUHAUS BUILT
- LINDBERGH FLIES THE ATLANTIC
- *THE JAZZ SINGER* HITS THE SCREEN
- MICKEY MOUSE IS BORN
- PENICILLIN DISCOVERED
- WALL STREET CRASH
- ZEPPELIN FLIES ROUND WORLD

WORLD POPULATION: 1,834 MILLION

THE TWENTIES START ROARING

The 1920s kick off with prohibition in the United States. Banning the manufacture and sale of alcohol leads to an unprecedented crime wave. The Treaty of Trianon redraws the map of Europe and the former Ottoman Empire is split into protectorates policed by France and Britain. The Netherlands begins a literal expansion plan by reclaiming land from the Zuider Zee. Marcus Garvey raises black consciousness in the United States when he establishes the Universal Negro Improvement Association. In Czechoslovakia, the robot is born.

OPPOSITE: Civic guards take a break during street demonstrations in Berlin.

1920

Jan	16	Prohibition of alcohol goes into force in the United States	July	9	Greek forces, with U.K. approval, capture Bursa in Asian Turkey
Feb	20	U.S. polar explorer Robert Peary dies at age 63	Aug	10	Treaty of Sèvres robs Turkey of 80 percent of the Ottoman Empire
				14	Olympic Games open in Antwerp, Belgium
Mar	15	U.S. Senate refuses to ratify the Treaty of Versailles for a second time			
			Sep	28	Eight Chicago White Sox players are charged with gambling on the 1919 World Series
Apr	7	French troops occupy Germany's Ruhr			
	25	League of Nations awards Middle East mandates to U.K. and France	Nov	16	Civil war in Russia ends after three years
					QANTAS airline set up in Australia
May	30	Pope Benedict declares Joan of Arc a saint		21	In Ireland, the IRA kills 14 British soldiers, the first "Bloody Sunday"
June	4	Treaty of Trianon redraws the map of Eastern Europe	Dec	10	Woodrow Wilson (1856–1924) is awarded the Nobel Prize for peace

MANDATES FOR FRANCE AND GREAT BRITAIN

In April, at San Remo, Italy, the League of Nations gives France a mandate over Syria and Lebanon and Britain a mandate over Iraq and Palestine. They are all former Ottoman territories. Britain is thus free to abide by the Balfour Declaration of 1917 and allow Jews to settle in Palestine.

PEACE WITH TURKEY

In August, at Sèvres, France, a peace treaty is signed with the former Ottoman Empire, which cuts it back to one-fifth of its former size. The treaty is opposed by Turkey, which resents giving land to the Greeks.

ABOVE: Airmail service is introduced, using seaplanes which can land anywhere there is water.

END OF RUSSIAN CIVIL WAR

In November, the Red Army, under Trotsky, wins its final battle against counterrevolutionary forces in the Crimea, bringing an end to the three-year-old Russian civil war.

SOUND ON FILM

American scientist Lee de Forest invents a system of recording synchronized sound on a separate track on cinema film, to be "read" by a photoelectric cell.

THE TREATY OF TRIANON

In June, the Treaty of Trianon (Paris) is signed with Hungary, redrawing the map of Eastern Europe. Former Hungarian lands are divided between Czechoslovakia, Poland, Austria, Yugoslavia, and Italy, leaving Hungary a third of its former size. The treaty follows on from Versailles, St Germain, and Neuilly, which together have settled the frontiers of Germany and Austria-Hungary.

THE LITTLE ENTENTE

In August, Yugoslavia and Czechoslovakia sign a treaty of friendship known as the Little Entente. Romania will join in April 1921. The countries are united in their desire to keep the current borders in Eastern Europe and not to allow any revival of the Hapsburg empire in either Austria or Hungary.

THE AGE OF INNOCENCE

The greatest book of the American writer Edith Wharton (1861–1937) is a study of American high society at the turn of the century, showing how human values such as love can be destroyed by the obligation to stick to outdated moral codes. In it, Wharton condemns people "who dreaded scandal more than disease, who placed decency above courage."

BELOW: Prohibition starts and teams are sent to dismantle bars and drinking clubs all over America.

THE INKBLOT TEST

Swiss psychiatrist, Hermann Rorschach (1884–1922), develops a test by which the personality, intelligence, and emotional stability of patients can be assessed by analyzing their interpretations of random patterns made by inkblots.

BONJOUR CHERI

In the first of her mature novels, the French writer Colette (Sidonie Gabrielle Colette, 1873–1954) describes a liaison between a young man and an older woman. *Chéri* will be followed by many other books, remarkable for their vivid evocations of sights, sounds, and smells, and for their frank depictions of the lives of women in the France of her time.

QANTAS TAKES TO THE AIR

Queensland and Northern Territory Aerial Service (QANTAS) is set up as Australia's commercial airline on November 16.

BLACK POWER

Marcus Garvey, Jamaican editor of *The Negro World* published in New York City, leads the first meeting of the Universal Negro Improvement Association (UNIA) in August. On the agenda for discussion by 3,000 delegates from across the United States is a bill of rights for Negroes.

BABE RUTH SOLD
In January, the Boston Red Sox sell Babe Ruth to the New York Yankees for $125,000 in the most infamous transaction in American sports history. After the sale, the Red Sox will not win the World Series until 2004. It is attributed to the "Curse of the Bambino" and the Yankees will become the most successful team ever.

HUGH SELWYN MAUBERLEY
Mauberley, a collection of linked poems by the American poet Ezra Pound (1885–1972), describes the literary life of London just after World War I. For its classical and ironical style, its compression of language, and its use of allusion, it quickly becomes one of the most influential works of the modern movement in literature.

THE SEVENTH OLYMPIC GAMES
In August, the Seventh Olympiad is staged in Antwerp, Belgium. It is the sixth actually held, as there were no Games in 1916. The Olympic flag of five linked rings, symbolizing the continents, is used for the first time. American diver Aileen Riggin became the youngest winner at 14.

LAND FROM THE SEA
The Wieringen Polder, the greatest-ever land reclamation scheme, begins in the Netherlands. Embankments built from over one million cubic feet of earth taken from the Zuider Zee will join north Holland to the Island of Wieringen, and that to Friesland.

THE TATLIN MONUMENT
Soviet artist Vladimir Tatlin (1885–1953) designs a great construction project which evokes technology and social progress in an upward-spiralling form containing cylinders and a glass pyramid. Although the monument is never built, and is known only in the form of a model, it is a lasting symbol of the kind of art embraced by the Soviet Union in its early years.

ABOVE: British troops are sent in to impose order on the streets of Londonderry where Sinn Féin and the Unionists are fighting.

RUR: THE BIRTH OF THE ROBOT
Karel Capek's play (the initials stand for Rossum's Universal Robots) introduces the word "robot" into the vocabulary. The robots are part of an anti-utopia, in which people try to use machines to improve their lot, but the machines are so effective that they take over and dominate their creators.

RADIO CONTACT
The first U.S. commercial broadcasting station, Pittsburgh KDKA, begins regular weekly broadcasts in November by announcing the Harding-Cox presidential election results. The new station, run by the Westinghouse Co., is also opening in France, Germany, and Argentina.

ENTER THE TOMMY-GUN
U.S. gunsmith John T. Thompson patents a sub-machine gun, which later becomes known as the tommy-gun.

OLIVE SCHREINER
(1855–1920)

The writer, pacifist, and feminist Olive Schreiner, whose husband was persuaded to take her name when they married in 1894, has died. Born of a German father and English mother in South Africa, where she spent most of her life, she published her first book, *The Story of an African Farm* (1883,) under the name Ralph Iron. Works under her own name include *Trooper Peter Halket* (1897) and *Woman and Labor* (1911).

NO MORE DRINKING

On January 16 it becomes illegal to manufacture, sell and transport intoxicating liquor in the United States when the Volstead Act, the 18th Amendment to the U.S. Constitution ratified on January 29, 1919, comes into effect.

LEGAL ABORTION

Abortion becomes legal for the first time in a modern European state, in legislation introduced in Russia. Since 1918 the new Bolshevik government has made marriage a civil ceremony, facilitated divorce, and introduced free maternity care. The new Czechoslovakia also legalizes abortion this year.

A NEW SAINT

Pope Benedict XV declares Joan of Arc a saint.

ROBERT EDWIN PEARY
(1856–1920)

The American naval commander and explorer Robert Edwin Peary, believed to be the first man to reach the North Pole in 1909, and veteran of eight Arctic expeditions, has died. The region of Greenland, Peary Land, is named in his honor.

BELOW: A nail bomb explodes outside the U.S. Assay Office on Wall Street, under the gaze of George Washington. Over 300 people are injured and 35 killed, but no perpetrator is ever found.

THE RISE OF FASCISM AND COMMUNISM

There is mutiny and economic collapse in Russia. In China, the young Mao Zedong helps to establish Communism. The Irish Free State is ratified, dividing the island. Marie Stopes introduces birth control to the U.K. In the U.S.A., heavyweight Jack Dempsey knocks out Georges Carpentier. Two inventions will be widely used: the Band-aid and the lie detector. The first woman priest is ordained. In Italy, Mussolini becomes Il Duce and Enrico Caruso's singing comes to an end.

OPPOSITE: Crowds outside the Kremlin display religious icons as well as red flags.

1921

Jan	6	Release of *The Kid*, Charlie Chaplin's first feature film
	21	Tanks patrol Dublin in search of IRA snipers
Mar	12	Lenin relaxes strict controls on Russia's economy
	17	Russia's Red Army crushes anti-Bolshevik rebellion at Kronstadt naval base
Apr	12	President Warren Harding says the United States will not join the League of Nations
June	22	In Ireland, King George V opens the first Ulster parliament
	30	First meeting of China's Communist Party is held
July	14	Sacco and Vanzetti are convicted of murder
July	27	Insulin has been isolated from the pancreas and will hopefully save the lives of diabetics
Aug	2	Italian tenor Enrico Caruso dies at 48
	5	Mustafa Kemal becomes virtual ruler of Turkey
Nov	5	Crown Prince Hirohito of Japan becomes regent for his father
	7	Benito Mussolini becomes head of Italy's National Fascist Party with the title of Il Duce, "the Leader"
Dec	7	Peace in Ireland: 26 southern counties become independent while six northern counties stay in the United Kingdom
	10	Albert Einstein wins the Nobel Prize for physics
	16	French composer Camille Saint-Saëns dies at age 86

MUTINY AND ECONOMIC COLLAPSE IN RUSSIA

In March, Russian sailors mutiny at the Kronstadt naval base (Petrograd, once St Petersburg) in protest of the new Communist government's policies. The sailors demand free elections and other reforms. The mutiny shakes the government, as the sailors were originally in the forefront of the revolution.

At the same time, in Moscow, Lenin announces to the Communist Party Congress that he is relaxing controls over the economy, ending state planning and encouraging private enterprise. The move is forced on Lenin because of the collapse in the economy as a result of the civil war.

CHINA TURNS RED

In July, the Chinese Communist Party holds its first meeting. It elects Chen Duxiu, a Beijing university professor, as its first president. Among its founding members is Mao Zedong.

EINSTEIN TOWER, POTSDAM

Designed by German Erich Mendelsohn (1887–1953), this building houses an observatory and laboratory. It is designed in a wholly "plastic" form, consisting almost completely of curves, and owes nothing to previous styles. The original intention was for the building to be constructed from poured concrete, but it is actually built of brick covered with cement.

A FREE STATE FOR IRELAND

In December, Irish Republican negotiators finally agree to a settlement with the British government, setting up an independent Free State in the south of Ireland. The British government decided in 1920 to divide Ireland, offering home rule to both the Catholic and Republican south and to the Protestant and Unionist north, but the south refused to accept limited home rule. The settlement comes after three years of vicious civil war in the south.

PROKOFIEV'S FIRST HIT

Russian composer Sergei Prokofiev (1891–1955) attends the premiere of his Piano Concerto No. 3. It is one of the most important and most popular works from his early Russian period. It helps establish him as a composer with his own distinctive style.

A MILLION DOLLAR GATE

In July, Jack "The Idol" Dempsey knocks out Frenchman Georges "The Orchid Kid" Carpentier in front of 80,000 fans. The heavyweight championship bout is the first million dollar gate in boxing and boosts boxing's popularity enormously.

FAST FIRST AID

Band-aid, the first stick-on bandage, is introduced in the U.S.A. by Johnson & Johnson.

LEFT: Mountaineer Captain Finch nears the summit of Mont Blanc, the giant of the French Alps.

ABOVE: President of the Irish Republic, Eamonn de Valera, is invited by Lloyd George to try to answer the Irish Question.

WAR IN THE AEGEAN

In January, war breaks out between Greece and Turkey, with the Greeks invading western Anatolia on the shores of the Aegean Sea. Fighting between the two countries continues in the region into 1922. It is home to many thousands of ethnic Greeks.

FIRST LIE DETECTOR

U.S. medical student John Larson invents the world's first lie detector. It shows by means of heart rate, breathing rate and blood pressure, if a subject is under stress when not telling the truth.

A HOUSEBOAT IN AMSTERDAM

Dutch architect Michel de Klerk, a member of the Amsterdam School, designs Het Scheep housing complex, notable for its decorative use of brickwork, tiling, and a variety of window shapes and glazing arrangements. Its nickname, meaning "the ship", derives from its wedge shape.

BIRTH CONTROL IN THE U.K.

In March, Marie Stopes (1880–1958) opens the U.K.'s first birth control clinic in London amid great opposition from the Establishment. In 1918 she published *Married Love*, the first sex education manual, and *Wise Parenthood*, which advocated birth control and sex education for women.

ABOVE: Georges Carpentier wilts under the onslaught of champion Jack Dempsey.

BELOW: Suzanne Lenglen and Bill Tilden play to victory in the Wimbledon Mixed Doubles.

UNITED STATES COAST TO COAST
In February, Lieutenant William D. Coney of the U.S. Air Force makes the first coast-to-coast flight across North America from California to Florida.

FIRST EXPRESSWAY
The world's first express highway, the Avus Autobahn, is opened in Berlin, foreshadowing the Autobahn network to be built in the 1930s.

ENRICO CARUSO
(1873–1921)

The world-renowned Italian tenor Enrico Caruso has died in Naples. He leaves a wealth of gramophone recordings to ensure that his voice will be appreciated by future generations. His first performance was in Naples in 1895, and international fame came in 1902 when he sang in *La Bohème* with Dame Nelly Melba at Monte Carlo. He made over 600 appearances and sang some 40 roles at the Met in New York, where he held his final performance on Christmas Eve in 1920.

ABOVE: Queen Wilhemina of the Netherlands, Prince Hendrik and Princess Juliana make an informal canal tour of their country.

FIRST WOMAN PRIEST
Rev. Antoinette Brown Blackwell becomes the first woman to be ordained in the Anglican Church in the U.S.

LYSOZYME DISCOVERED
Scottish bacteriologist Alexander Fleming (1881–1955) discovers the existence of lysozyme, an enzyme present in saliva, tears, and nasal mucus. It helps to kill bacteria naturally and to prevent infection.

SEXUAL REFORM
The World League for Sexual Reform is set up in Berlin by Magnus Hirschfeld, a homosexual doctor. In 1919, he founded the Institute for Sex Research in Berlin.

GAMES FOR WOMEN
In Monte Carlo, the first Women's World Games are held in protest of women not being allowed to take part in Olympic track and field events.

ABOVE: The first glimpse into an Egyptian tomb unearthed near
Thebes creates excavation fever that grips the decade.

SECRETS FROM AN EGYPTIAN TOMB

A year of alliance and excavation: Russia and its satellites become the mighty U.S.S.R., and Germany makes an alliance with the Soviets. Mussolini seizes power in Italy. The ancient city of Ur is unearthed in Iraq. In Egypt, the tomb of the young Tutankhamun yields its secrets. Retail sales enter a new arena when the first shopping mall is introduced in the United States. Insulin use succeeds for the first time. In Ireland, Michael Collins is shot dead. French novelist Marcel Proust eats his last madeleine. Alexander Bell, inventor of the telephone, finally hangs up!

OPPOSITE: Mask of Tutankhamun, whose tomb is discovered this year.

1922

Jan	5	British explorer Ernest Shackleton dies at age 49
	11	A diabetic in Toronto, Canada is being successfulyl treated with the new drug insulin
Feb	5	The first issue of *The Reader's Digest* is published in the United States
Mar	18	Mahatma Gandhi is jailed for civil discontent
Apr	16	German and Soviet Russia sign a secret treaty
	21	Alessandro Moreschi, the last known castrato, dies
Aug	2	Telephone inventor Alexander Graham Bell dies at age 75
	14	British newspaper owner Viscount Northcliffe dies at age 57
Aug	22	In Ireland, Sinn Féin leader Michael Collins is shot dead at age 32
Sep	4	U.S. aviator James H. Doolittle flies from Florida to California in one day
Oct	15	Treaty of Mudania ends the war between Greece and Turkey
	30	Benito Mussolini and the Fascists take power in Italy
Nov	15	British Broadcasting Company broadcasts its first wireless news bulletin
	26	The tomb of the Egyptian pharaoh Tutankhamun is found in Egypt
Dec	10	Niels Bohr of Denmark wins the Nobel Prize in physics
	30	Soviet Russia changes its name to the Union of Soviet Socialist Republics

ABOVE: A huge explosion rocks the Four Courts in Dublin, the result of a mine. Thirty Free State troopers are killed in the explosion and fighting continues for four hours afterwards.

ABOVE: Leader of the IRA Michael Collins speaking at Armagh. He is later shot and killed in the Irish civil war.

GERMAN AND SOVIET ALLIANCE

In April, Germany and Soviet Russia sign a secret peace treaty at Rapallo, Italy, under which they reestablish full diplomatic and trading relations, agree to waive reparations payments, and commit to full co-operation between their armed forces. The treaty shocks Europe, as it allows Germany a way of rebuilding her army in defiance of the Versailles Treaty.

IL DUCE SEIZES POWER

In Rome, 24,000 members of the Italian Fascist Party march from Naples to Rome to seize power. Their leader, Benito Mussolini, waits in Milan, ready to flee to Switzerland if the coup fails. However, there is no opposition in Rome and King Victor Emmanuel asks Mussolini to form a government.

RUSSIA BECOMES U.S.S.R.

Russia formally changes its name and becomes the Union of the Soviet Socialist Republics, a confederation with Belarus, Ukraine, and the Transcaucasian Federation.

THE WASTE LAND

The major work of the American poet T.S. Eliot (1888–1965) uses imagery from myth and past literature to evoke the desolation of modern humanity and the breakdown of modern values and belief systems. Its mixture of styles, ranging from everyday Cockney speech to literary allusion and quotation, baffles but impresses its first readers.

COLLINS SHOT

The Irish prime minister, Michael Collins, is assassinated in County Cork by opponents of the treaty signed with Britain last December. Although the Irish parliament accepted the treaty in January, opponents have taken up arms against their former friends and civil war is now raging throughout the Free State.

TALES OF ULYSSES

Irish writer James Joyce's groundbreaking novel is published. It incorporates major innovations in the use of interior monologue, cinematic scene-setting, and language. It will be valued for these modernist features and also for its realistic portrayal of its main characters, for its humor, and for its vivid depiction of Dublin. Because of alleged obscenity, the book is printed in Dijon and published in Paris.

AIRCRAFT CARRIER

The USS *Langley* becomes the first U.S. aircraft carrier. She is converted from a coal ship, the *Jupiter*.

DISCOVERY OF INSULIN

In February, a group of Canadian scientists, Frederick Banting, Charles Best, James Collip, and Professor John Macleod, jointly announce the discovery of insulin and detail its use in treating diabetes.

ABOVE: The New Lincoln Memorial is a huge but benign statue of Abraham Lincoln by American sculptor Daniel Chester French.

THE EARLIEST CITY

Ur, an ancient city on the River Euphrates in Iraq, is excavated by a British Museum and University of Pennsylvania expedition headed by Charles Leonard Woolley (1880–1960), the English archaeologist who has just excavated the ancient Egyptian site of Tel-el-Amarna. The discovery of a Sumerian temple proves that Ur flourished in Mesopotamia as early as 2600 BC.

IMPERIAL HOTEL, TOKYO

Asked to design a building that will withstand earthquakes, architect Frank Lloyd Wright (1869–1959) develops a system of concrete posts which support the structure while allowing it to "give" during an earthquake. About two years after completion, the building is shaken by a severe quake, but remains standing and provides a refuge for those left homeless.

SAVING THE KOALA

The koala bear, a native marsupial found only in Australia, is now protected by rigidly strict legislation. Fur trappers have killed some eight million animals over the last four years alone.

IMMORTALIZING THE LIVING DEAD

Nosferatu, the first major vampire movie, is also the first major film directed by F.W. Murnau. It includes effects such as negative imagery (black appearing as white and vice versa) to intensify the atmosphere of strangeness and horror. Many imitators will follow in its wake.

PEACE BETWEEN TURKEY AND GREECE

The war between Greece and Turkey ends when they sign the Treaty of Mudania. Greece withdraws from Anatolia and the area around Constantinople. As a result, the British wartime leader, David Lloyd George, loses power as prime minister and is replaced by the Conservative leader Andrew Bonar-Law.

SOUND-ON-FILM MOVIE

The first commercial sound-on-film motion picture is *Der Brandstifter* (*The Arsonist*) made in Germany. But it does not immediately lead to the end of silent films.

TUTANKHAMUN COMES TO LIGHT

The tomb containing the sarcophagus of the ancient Egyptian boy king, Tutankhamun, who reigned during the Eighteenth Dynasty (fourteenth century BC), is discovered in November by two British archaeologists, Howard Carter and his sponsor, the Earl of Carnarvon.

MARCEL PROUST
(1871–1922)

One of the most influential writers of modern times, the French novelist Marcel Proust, has died. Born in Paris where he spent his life, he was a semi-invalid and lived his last seventeen years writing reclusively in his apartment. His thirteen volume work *A la Recherche du Temps Perdu* (translated into English as *Remembrance of Times Past*) has won great acclaim. The second volume won the Prix Goncourt in 1919 and an international reputation followed. At the time of his death, three final volumes are awaiting publication.

ALEXANDER GRAHAM BELL
(1847–1922)

Alexander Graham Bell, the inventor of the telephone and founder of the Bell Telephone Company (1877) has died. This American, of Scottish birth and education, established a training school in Boston for teachers of deaf people and later became Professor of Vocal Physiology. The telephone sprang from experiments with acoustical devices to aid deaf and dumb people. His other interest was aeronautics.

MR. LINCOLN COMES TO WASHINGTON
The Lincoln Memorial, Washington D.C., becomes a place of national pilgrimage with the completion of Daniel Chester French's memorial statue.

DAY TRIP
Lieutenant James H. Doolittle makes the first one day flight across the United States from Florida to California; time 22 hours and 35 minutes, including a refuelling stop.

ABOVE: The largest telescope in the world at Mount Wilson in California. It incorporates an instrument for measuring the diameter of stars and is to be significant in the discovery of galaxies.

RETAIL SALES
The world's first shopping mall, the Country Club Plaza, opens in the United States in July.

DANISH SUCCESS
Danish scientist Niels Bohr wins Nobel Prize for physics.

FIRST GLIMPSES OF NAZISM AND HITLER

Nazism rears its head when the first rally is held in Munich. At the same time, French troops occupy the Ruhr, impatient at the slow delivery of war reparations. The German mark collapses. Turkey becomes a republic, signaling the death of the once mighty Ottoman Empire. Far from the troubled Earth, galaxies and nebulae are discovered. A Spanish engineer flies the first rotor-driven flight machine. French actress Sarah Bernhardt takes her final curtain call.

1923

Jan	25	French troops march into Germany's Ruhr to collect war reparations
	27	The first National Socialist (Nazi) rally is held in Munich, Germany
Feb	10	German X-ray discoverer Wilhelm Roentgen dies at age 77
Mar	9	Russian leader V.I. Lenin suffers a stroke and there is speculation about who will be chosen to be his successor as leader of the Soviet Union
	26	Legendary French actress Sarah Bernhardt dies at 78
Apr	28	Wembley Stadium, London, hosts its first football cup final
Aug	2	U.S. president Warren Harding dies at age 69; he is succeeded by Vice President Calvin Coolidge
Aug	12	Italian Enrico Triboschi swims the English Channel in a record 16 hours 33 minutes
Sep	1	An earthquake destroys Tokyo and Yokohama in Japan. At least 140,000 die and two million are homeless
Oct	29	Mustafa Kemal proclaims a republic in Turkey, with himself as president
Nov	12	Adolf Hitler tries to seize power in Bavaria, Germany, and is arrested
	15	German mark collapses to 20,142 billion per pound sterling; a loaf of bread costs 201 billion marks
Dec	7	British general election results in a "hung" Parliament
	28	French engineer Gustav Eiffel dies at 91

ABOVE: A violent earthquake devastates Tokyo, destroying most of the city center and killing 140,000 people.

THE "SICK MAN OF EUROPE" DIES

In October, the Ottoman Empire finally collapses when Mustafa Kemal, a leading Nationalist politician, proclaims Turkey a republic and himself as president. The new peace treaty with Greece and the allies, signed at Lausanne in July, restores much territory to Turkey.

THE FIRST FOOTBALL CUP FINAL

In April, the English Football Association Cup Final at Wembley Stadium in London is won by the Bolton Wanderers 2–0 over West Ham. "The White Horse Final" will be remembered, however, for the huge crowd that swarms to the first game to be played at the stadium. Spectators fill the stadium to the very edge of the playing surface and have to be marshaled by mounted police.

WILHELM KONRAD VON ROENTGEN (1845–1923)

The German winner of the first Nobel Prize for physics in 1901, Wilhelm Roentgen has died. In 1895 he discovered X-rays, or electromagnetic rays. He also achieved important results in the study of heat in gases and crystals, and in dielectrics (substances that do not conduct electricity).

FRANCISCO (PANCHO) VILLA (1877–1923)

The Mexican revolutionary, Pancho Villa, has been murdered in Parral. Born Doroteo Arango, son of a field laborer, he became a military commander during the Mexican Revolution and continued as a guerrilla fighter after his defeat in 1915. He made a truce with the government in 1920.

THE COSTS OF WAR

In January, French and Belgian troops occupy the industrialized Ruhr region to seize coal, timber, steel, and other reparations owed to them by Germany as part of the peace treaty that ended the war. The Germans respond with strikes, acts of sabotage, and street protests. French troops remain in the region until July 1925.

FIRST AUTOGIRO FLIGHTS

Spanish aeroengineer Juan de la Cierva makes the first successful flight in an autogiro, an aircraft with a free-wheeling rotor that acts as the wing.

BELOW: A member of archaeologist Lord Carnarvon's team on the trail of new treasures from Egypt.

LEFT: The Great Citroën Expedition across the Sahara encounters a desert warrior using more traditional transport. The desert terrain is a great test of the car's abilities.

LOUIS MARIE ANN COUPERUS
(1863–1923)

Louis Couperus, the Dutch poet and novelist, has died. His first novel, *Eline Vere*, written in the new naturalistic style, was published in 1889 and this was followed by several others set in the Dutch East Indies, where he grew up, and a tetralogy (1901–1904), *Dr. Adriaan* (translated into English as *The Books of Small Souls*), set in The Hague.

THE BEER HALL PUTSCH
The National Socialist Party, or Nazis, led by Adolf Hitler, attempts a coup in Munich against the German government by trying to seize control in Bavaria. It fails and Hitler is sent to prison.

HEAT CONTROL
The thermostat begins a revolution in the efficiency of domestic appliances when it is fitted to a New World gas cooker in Britain. Commercial companies seek to exploit its potential for regulating electric cookers, electric irons, kettles, and water heaters.

MONEY FOR NOTHING
In November, the German mark collapses, losing so much value that its exchange rate falls to 4,200,000 billion marks to the dollar. As prices soar, the German government issues a new currency, the Rentenmark, at a level of 4.2 to the dollar.

GALAXIES GALORE
U.S. astronomer Edwin Powell Hubble (1889–1953) discovers that the Andromeda nebula lies outside the boundary of our own galaxy. This discovery leads to the realization that each nebula is a separate galaxy.

ELECTRONIC CAMERA TUBE
Russian-born electronics engineer Vladimir Zworykin (1889–1982) invents the iconoscope, the first electronic camera tube.

CONCRETE SPACE
Airship hangars at Orly, Paris, designed by French civil engineer and concrete expert Eugène Freyssinet, show how steel and concrete construction can be used to create enormous spaces. The great parabolic concrete vaults are 197 feet high and 574 feet long. The vaults get their strength from their ridged construction, similar to corrugated cardboard.

THE GOOD SOLDIER SCHWEIK
This unfinished masterpiece by Jaroslav Hasek is based on the author's experiences in the Austro-Czech Army in 1915. It portrays an anarchic, anti-authoritarian, even antisocial Czech "hero," who ridicules his Austrian masters. Schweik becomes a symbol of all those who struggle as individuals against oppressive political systems.

AN EARLY SUPERMARKET
A precursor of the supermarket opens in San Francisco. Called the Crystal Palace, it sells food, drugs, cigarettes, and jewelry. It also includes a barber shop, a ladies hair and beauty salon, and a dry cleaner.

THEY SHOOT HORSES DON'T THEY?
In the wake of the Depression and huge unemployment, the craze for marathon dancing hits the United States. Couples dance until they drop to win cash prizes.

SARAH-MARIE-HENRIETTE ROSINE BERNHARDT
(1844–1923)

The French actress Sarah Bernhardt, who was born Sarah-Marie-Henriette Rosine Bernard in Paris in 1844, has died. After 14 years on the Paris stage, she first became internationally known in 1876. Famous for her tragic roles, such as Phèdre in Racine's play of the same name, she founded her own theater in 1899. Despite having a leg amputated in 1915, she continued to give stage performances in France, the United States, London, and other European cities.

THE RISE AND RISE OF ADOLF HITLER

The Nazis begin their unrelenting rise in Germany as members of the party are elected to the Reichstag. In Russia, Lenin dies. Perhaps in response to an increasingly complex world, the Surrealist Manifesto is declared by French artist and poet André Breton. On the domestic scene, spin driers, frozen food, and refrigerators are introduced. The first Winter Olympics takes place in the French Alps and "Big Bill" Tilden wins his fifth consecutive U.S. national tennis championship.

1924

Jan	21	Russian leader Vladimir Lenin dies at 54
	23	Britain has its first Labour government, led by Ramsay MacDonald
	27	In Moscow, Lenin's boby is laid to rest in a marble tomb near the Kremlin
	31	First International Winter Sports Week is held at Chamonix, France; it is later called the Winter Olympics
Feb	12	U.S. pianist George Gershwin gives the first performance of his *Rhapsody in Blue*
Apr	1	Adolf Hitler is sentenced to five years for treason for his role in a revolt at a Munich beer hall
May	4	The first Nazis are elected to the German Reichstag (Parliament)

June	2	First wireless conversation between Britain and Australia takes place
	3	Czech author Franz Kafka dies at 40
July	5	The Eighth Olympic Games open in Paris
Aug	3	Author Joseph Conrad dies at 66
	16	London conference adopts the Dawes Plan to help Germany pay its war reparations
	24	British liner *Mauretania* sets a new Blue Riband record for crossing the Atlantic: 5 days 1 hour 35 minutes
Nov	4	French composer Gabriel Fauré dies at age 79
	29	Italian composer Giacomo Puccini dies at age 65
Dec	20	Adolf Hitler is released from jail on parole

ABOVE: Adolf Hitler is jailed, then released, and begins his rise to power in Germany.

THOMAS WOODROW WILSON
(1856–1924)

Woodrow Wilson, the 28th American president (1913–1921) and winner of the Nobel Prize for peace in 1919, has died. President Wilson reluctantly led the United States into World War I in 1917 and helped to bring the war to an end. A Democrat, he was instrumental in forming the League of Nations, which the Senate then prevented the United States from joining.

DEATH OF LENIN

Vladimir Ilyich Lenin, the founder of the Soviet Union, dies in Moscow at age 54. He had suffered the first of three strokes in May 1922 and control of the government had been passed to other people, notably Joseph Stalin, general secretary of the Communist Party.

FIRST BRITISH LABOUR GOVERNMENT

A Labour government takes power in Britain for the first time ever. Led by Ramsay MacDonald, the Labour government is supported in power by the Liberals, but soon collapses and loses in the general election called in October.

NAZIS BECOME ESTABLISHMENT

In May, the Nazis enter the Reichstag, the German Parliament, for the first time by taking 32 seats in the general election. The Social Democrats remain the largest party, but both the Nationalists and Communists gain ground.

SURREALISTS SHOW THEMSELVES

French writer André Breton (1896–1966) publishes his Manifesto to mark the official beginning of the surrealist movement. It aims to break down the distinctions between dream and reality and madness and rationality in all forms of art.

A PASSAGE TO INDIA

English writer E.M. Forster (1879–1970) publishes what is probably his greatest book, the last of his novels to be published in his lifetime. A picture of life in India under British rule, the book lays bare the prejudices that both Britons and Indians have about each other and the clashes that result.

LIVING IN STIJL

With its white walls, clean lines, and primary color details, the Schröder-Schräder house, Utrecht, designed by Gerrit Rietveld, is a classic example of De Stijl design. The right angle is everywhere in this building. Even the windows can only be opened so that they are at 90 degrees to the facade.

GOODBYE TO WASHDAY BLUES

The spin drier, consisting of a spinning drum built into a washing machine which extracts water by centrifugal force, is produced by the Savage Arms Corporation in the United States and used to help dry wet clothes.

GERMANY SETTLES HER DEBTS

Germany and the Allies accept the Dawes Report to settle the issue of reparations by establishing a plan for annual payments. As a result, the German Reichsbank introduces a new mark to stabilize the economy, which is supported by a foreign loan.

QUICK-FROZEN FOOD

Birds Eye Seafoods launches the first commercially produced fast-frozen food. U.S. fur trader Clarence Birdseye (1886–1956) experimented with preserving perishable foods by freezing, after visiting Labrador in 1917 and eating palatable fish that had been preserved in ice. Now he sets up a company to produce quick-frozen food for the retail market.

CONTROVERSY ON STAGE

Paul Robeson and Mary Blair play an interracial couple in *All God's Chillun Got Wings* by American dramatist Eugene O'Neill (1888–1953). It is a controversial play attacking racism.

MY LIFE IN ART

Konstantin Stanislavsky (1865–1938), the great Russian director, looks back over his life and his experience in the theater. In the book he outlines various theories that have influenced the way many modern theater directors have approached their work. The Method becomes increasingly popular in the 1920s as the result of Stanislavsky's books.

PARTICLES = WAVES

French physicist Louis de Broglie discovers that electrons and other particles can behave as waves, as well as particles, thus becoming the founder of the science of wave mechanics.

JOSEPH CONRAD (JOZEF TEODOR KONRAD NALECZ KORZENIOWSKI)
(1857–1924)

The Polish-born naturalized British writer, Joseph Conrad, has died. At the age of 21 he joined a British merchant ship and six years later gained his master's certificate. He spent many years at sea but settled in Kent after his marriage in 1896. There, he became a writer using his experiences as inspiration. Among his best-known works are *Lord Jim* (1900), *Nostromo* (1904), *Heart of Darkness* (1902), and *Victory* (1919). He was working on a novel, *Suspense*, when he died.

RHAPSODY IN BLUE

American composer George Gershwin (1898–1937) writes this popular piece originally for Paul Whiteman's jazz band. It will later become better known in the form of an arrangement for classical symphony orchestras. The work is the first distinctively American piece of concert music, although if Charles Ives had been better known, the story would have been different.

THE SOUTHERN APE

Australian anthropologist Raymond Dart (1893–1988) discovers a skull in a South African quarry. It is a primitive hominid which Dart names Australopithecus (southern ape).

ELECTRIC REFRIGERATOR

Swedish engineers Balzer von Platen and Carl Munters patent the first refrigerator using an electric motor to drive the compressor. It is called the Electrolux.

WINTER OLYMPICS

In January, the International Winter Sports Week in Chamonix, France, is retrospectively declared the First Winter Olympics. The Scandinavians dominate the event, which is organized by the French Olympic Committee. The success of the event leads the International Olympic Committee to stage Winter Games in tandem with Summer Olympics.

AROUND THE WORLD FLIGHT

Two U.S. Douglas DCW biplanes, *Chicago* (piloted by Lieutenant Lowell H. Smith) and *New Orleans* (piloted by Lieutenant Erik Nelson), make the first around the world flight. It takes 175 days from April to September. Three other planes failed to make the full journey.

FRANZ KAFKA
(1883–1924)

The Czech writer of German-Jewish parentage, Franz Kafka, has died of tuberculosis in Berlin after many years of ill health. His novels, written in the German language, express the angst of the sensitive individual in a seemingly irrational society; the adjective "Kafkaesque" will soon be familiar to those who have not even read his books. The works include the short story "Metamorphosis" (1916) and the unfinished novels *The Trial*, *The Castle*, and *Amerika*, all to be published after his death.

ENTER KLEENEX

U.S. firm Kimberley Clark introduces the first tissues, called Celluwipes. They are now known as Kleenex™.

THE EIGHTH OLYMPIAD

Finnish athlete Paavo Nurmi wins five golds as the Olympics return to Paris for the Eighth Olympic Games. The Olympic Village, where athletes live, makes a return and events are broadcast on radio for the first time. Eric Liddell and Harold Abrahams, later to be immortalized in the film *Chariots of Fire*, win sprint medals for Britain.

FREE EDUCATION

An educational experiment is launched with the founding of Summerhill, a self-governing coeducational boarding school, by a British schoolmaster Alexander Sutherland Neil. Pupils are allowed to develop in their own way without the constraints of discipline, direction, or moral and religious instruction.

SWEDISH HEAT

The Aga, a cooker that uses solid fuel cleanly and has an efficient temperature control, is invented by Gustav Galen, a blind Swedish scientist.

HIGHWAY NETWORK

Italian companies begin building a 310 mile network of *autostrada*, toll highways. The first opens in September.

LEFT: Artists and writers in exile. James Joyce, Ezra Pound, Ford Maddox Ford, and John Quinn gather in Ezra Pound's Paris studio.

STALIN GETS A TIGHTER GRIP

Three men who will dominate the world are active this year. In the U.S.S.R., Stalin seizes power. In Germany, Hitler publishes *Mein Kampf*. In China, Chiang Kai-shek succeeds as leader of the People's Party. In the United States, the Scopes trial focuses on fundamentalism and evolution and the Ku Klux Klan march is unopposed by the establishment. Charlie Chaplin films *The Gold Rush* and Sergei Eisenstein films *Battleship Potemkin*. The first frisbee is thrown.

OPPOSITE: The Murrumbidgee River hits the Burrin Jack Dam during Australia's May floods.

1925

Jan	16	In Russia, Stalin dismisses Leon Trotsky as commissar for war
Mar	12	Dr. Sun Yat-sen, leader of the Kuomintang, China's People's Party, dies at age 69. He is succeeded by General Chiang Kai-shek
	23	State of Tennessee bans the teaching of evolution theory
Apr	25	Field Marshal Paul von Hindenburg is elected president of Germany
May	1	Cyprus becomes a British colony
July	18	Adolf Hitler's book *Mein Kampf (My Struggle)* is published
July	21	Biology teacher John Scopes is fined $100 in Tennessee for teaching evolution
Aug	16	Premiere of Charlie Chaplin's film *The Gold Rush*
Oct	16	Belgium, Britain, France, Germany, and Italy sign the Locarno Pact, promising to keep peace with one another
Nov	14	First Surrealist art exhibition in Paris includes work from Picasso and Klee
Dec	10	George Bernard Shaw is awarded the Nobel Prize for literature

THE LOCARNO PEACE

A major peace conference between Germany and the Allies agrees to a security pact for western and central Europe, guaranteeing frontiers and settling outstanding disputes. The treaty appears to guarantee peace between Germany and her former enemies.

NICARAGUAN CIVIL WAR

1925 sees the start of the civil war in Nicaragua. It will last until 1933. President Calles is opposed by three separate guerrilla groups led by Generals Moncada, Díaz, and Sandino. Díaz and Moncada eventually become allies, but Sandino remains independent. The United States backs the president and sends in the marines. General Sandino escapes to Guatemala, but returns when the marines leave. The war is eventually won by the presidential forces, but the rebel Sandinistas (named for General Sandino) keep up guerrilla warfare.

TROTSKY DISMISSED

Leon Trotsky is dismissed as commissar for war by Joseph Stalin and placed under house arrest. Many of his supporters are imprisoned or exiled to Siberia. The moves consolidate Stalin's grip on power in the Soviet Union after the death of Lenin.

THE GREAT GATSBY

F. Scott Fitzgerald (1896–1940) was already famous as a writer and representative of the "jazz age" when he published his greatest novel. It portrays the doomed passion of rich Jay Gatsby for Daisy Buchanan and evokes the sophistication and squalor of New York. The book is remarkable for describing the glamour and the dream of Gatsby, showing the hollowness of this vision as it turns to dust, and yet convincing us that the dream does have some value after all.

GERMANY ELECTS A PRESIDENT

In April, Field Marshal Paul von Hindenburg becomes the first directly elected German president. Hindenburg is supported by right wing and nationalist parties, many of which want to see the German monarchy restored.

COSMIC RAYS

U.S. physicist Robert Millikan (1868–1953) coins the term "cosmic rays" for radiation from outer space.

RUDOLF STEINER
(1861–1925)

Rudolf Steiner, the Croatian-born Austrian and founder of the Anthroposophical Society in 1912, has died. Influenced by theosophy, he believed that our spiritual development has been blocked by modern materialism. Many Steiner schools for children have developed since his founding of the first one in 1919.

ERIK ALFRED LESLIE SATIE
(1866–1925)

The French composer Erik Satie, whose mother was Scottish, has died in Paris. After training at the Paris Conservatoire, he first earned his living as a pianist in a Montmartre cabaret. His compositions for the piano, such as *Gymnopédies* (1888) and *Three Pear-shaped Pieces* (1903), were eccentric and avant-garde. He composed the music for the Diaghilev ballet *Parade* in 1917 and was part of the circle of surrealists and dadaists.

DRINKING IN STIJL

Designed by JJP Oud, the Café De Unie in Rotterdam is a De Stijl building that makes a bold statement. In a city street flanked by two old, traditional-style buildings, its brightly colored facade and bold sans-serif signage shine out as symbolic of the modern era.

THE FIRST FRISBEE

The frisbee is improvised by Yale University students using tin plates meant to hold pies baked by the Frisbie Baking Company of Bridgeport, Connecticut. An aerodynamically designed version is later marketed as a game.

THE TRIAL

Franz Kafka's novel is published a year after his death. It is the story of Josef K., caught in a labyrinth of law and officialdom and powerless to escape or control his fate. More than any other of Kafka's books, it has given us the term "Kafkaesque" for this situation.

THE BATTLESHIP POTEMKIN

The brutalities of the czarist regime are dramatized in Sergei Eisenstein's landmark film about a mutiny during the 1905 revolution. Eisenstein's most famous work shows the effectiveness of his technique of montage, a method of editing that boldly exploits visual metaphor.

BETTER VACUUM PACKS

Thermos vacuum flasks covered in plastic go on sale. They are lighter, longer-lasting, and cheaper than their predecessors, patented in 1902 by a German, Reinhold Burger. These were large, cumbersome, fragile, and rather expensive because they were covered in nickel.

THE RISE OF THE KLAN

The Ku Klux Klan suffers a setback when its Kentucky leader, D.C. Stephenson, is imprisoned for assault, rape, and kidnapping. The Klan's political power and membership have grown in recent years. Over 40,000 members attend its first national congress on August 8, complete with a parade through Washington, D.C.

SCOPES TRIAL

Science teacher John T. Scopes faces trial in July for violating a state law in Tennessee forbidding the teaching of evolutionary theory. He is convicted and fined $100, but cleared on appeal. The state law will be repealed in 1967.

ELECTRICITY METER

U.S. electrical engineer Vannevar Bush devises the first induction watt-hour meter for measuring electricity. Such meters are now found in homes all over the world.

ALL FALL DOWN

Engineers report that the famous leaning tower of Pisa will eventually fall down, but give no date for this.

THE GOLDRUSH

Charles Chaplin writes, produces, directs, and plays the part of the Tramp in this film. This is one of many features he makes with United Artists. The unique combination of humor, pathos, and resilience of his tramp character makes his films popular.

MEIN KAMPF PUBLISHED

Hitler publishes *Mein Kampf* (*My Struggle*), written while he was in jail and containing the main tenets of his Nationalist-Socialist philosophy, including the idea of *Lebensraum*, the expansion of German territory.

BELOW: A new design of parachute, the seat-pack. It is designed in America and favored by the air stunt artists who perform in shows all over the United States and Europe.

A YEAR OF STRIKE AND DISCONTENT

In England, the General Strike paralyzes and polarizes the country. The North Pole receives two flying visits: one by plane and one by airship. Saudi Arabia is established as a country. Germany joins the League of Nations. At Dessau, Walter Gropius erects the first Bauhaus, the seminal school of art and architecture. Hearts are broken as Rudolph Valentino dies and the art world mourns as Claude Monet comes to the end of a long and prolific career at the easel.

OPPOSITE: Mussolini addresses a crowd in Rome hours after a failed assassination attempt.

1 9 2 6

Jan	6	German airline Lufthansa is founded
	8	In Arabia, Ibn Saud is proclaimed King of the Hejaz
	27	Scottish inventor John Logie Baird gives the first demonstration of television
Mar	6	Robert A. Goddard launches the first liquid-fuel rocket
Apr	30	In Britain, coal miners go on strike; the strike lasts until November
May	5	Britain's first General Strike begins in support of the miners
	9	Richard Byrd and Floyd Bennett fly over the North Pole in an airplane
	12	General Strike in Britain ends, but the miners stay out
	13	Umberto Nobile, Roald Amundsen, and Lincoln Ellsworth fly over the North Pole

June	10	Spanish architect Antonio Gaudí is run over by a bus and killed
Aug	23	Screen heartthrob Rudolf Valentino dies at 31
Sep	8	League of Nations votes to admit Germany
Oct	14	A.A. Milne's *Winnie-the-Pooh* is published
	23	In Russia, Stalin expels Leon Trotsky and Grigori Zinoviev from the Politburo
Nov	20	Canada, Australia, South Africa, and Newfoundland become self-governing dominions, with Great Britain as head of the newly formed Commonwealth
Dec	5	French artist Claude Monet dies at 86

ABOVE: Armored cars in London guard the food trucks driven by strike breakers during the General Strike that grips the country.

THE BIRTH OF SAUDI ARABIA
Ibn Saud is proclaimed King of the Hejaz at Mecca. This marks the end of a long struggle by the Saud family to control the Arabian peninsula. Further conquest will result in the kingdom of Saudi Arabia in 1932.

BRITAIN'S STRIKING MINERS
A General Strike is called by the Trades Union Congress to support the miners in the struggle with the coal owners over pay and conditions. The strike lasts for just over a week, but the miners continue to stay on strike until November, when they are forced to accept a longer working day and local rather than national bargaining in pay and conditions.

GERMANY JOINS THE LEAGUE
The League of Nations votes unanimously to admit Germany. However, both Russia and the United States remain outside the League, reducing its importance in international affairs.

DE VALERA AND THE FIANNA FAIL
The Republican leader, Éamon de Valera, who opposed the treaty setting up the Irish Free State, breaks with his hardline allies and forms Fianna Fáil, the "Soldiers of Destiny," to fight for power in Ireland. They enter the Dáil, the Irish parliament, for the first time in August 1927, ending a lengthy boycott by anti-treaty Republicans.

TROTSKY AND ZINOVIEV EXPELLED
Leon Trotsky and Grigori Zinoviev, chairman of Comintern, the Communist International Committee, are both expelled from the Politburo, the ruling committee of the Communist Party. Stalin now holds supreme power in the Soviet Union.

IS IT A BIRD?
Romanian sculptor Constantin Brancusi (1876–1957) exhibits his sculpture, *Bird in Space*. The degree of abstraction that sculpture has reached becomes a public talking point when the authorities in New York refuse to admit Brancusi's sculpture is a work of art and try to tax it as a piece of metal. There is a court case and the court finally accepts that it is art after all.

A NEW BAUHAUS, DESSAU
Walter Gropius (1883–1969) designs this landmark building for a landmark institution, which moves to Dessau after political pressure forces it to leave Weimar. The elegant but austere building, like the institution it houses, seems to unite art and industry. Inside, some of Europe's greatest artists and designers, such as Kandinsky, Moholy-Nagy, and Gropius, teach the arts of design and architecture and spread the ideals of modernism.

THE NEW DUTCH SCHOOL
The Vondelschool is built in Hilversum. Impressive for its sober, elegant use of brickwork and its strong horizontal lines, this is one of many such buildings by Dudok in the new town to the southeast of Amsterdam.

PIAGET'S THEORY
A pioneering study of children's mental development is published by Jean Piaget, a Swiss psychologist who studied under Jung and worked with Alfred Binet on children's intelligence tests. He theorizes that the development of mental processes is determined genetically and always occurs in four stages.

MEXICAN INSURRECTIONS 1926–1929
In this year, anticlerical provisions in the Mexican 1917 Constitution are implemented. Clerical land is seized, church property is nationalized, and bishops are exiled. A guerrilla group calling themselves the Cristoferos fight on the side of the clergy. There are no major outbreaks but many skirmishes. In 1929, agreement will be reached between the two parties.

CLAUDE MONET
(1840–1926)

The French impressionist painter Claude Monet, whose painting *Impression, Soleil Levant* exhibited in 1874 and initiated the term impressionism, has died. His technique was to build up a painting from patches of pure color. His paintings often consist of a series examining the same subject again and again in different lights, as in his *Argenteuil* series (1872–75), *Views of London* (1902), *Rouen Cathedral* (1892–95), and the countless *Water-lilies* (1899–1926).

FIRST T.V. DEMONSTRATED
In January, Scottish inventor John Logie Baird (1888–1946) demonstrates the first true television transmission to 50 scientists at the Royal Institution in London using a mechanical scanner.

NORGE OVER THE NORTH POLE
Italian aviator Umberto Nobile flies across the North Pole in his airship *Norge*, accompanied by explorers Roald Amundsen (Norway) and Lincoln Ellsworth (U.S.).

WATERPROOF WATCH
The first waterproof watch is made by the Rolex Company of Switzerland and marketed as the Oyster.

METROPOLIS
This important film by Austrian director Fritz Lang (1890–1976) uses the genre of science fiction to create a vision of a nightmare urban landscape, which influences many other moviemakers. Set in a mechanized, slave-served society in the year 2000, the film uses expressionistic sets and techniques to depict the horrors of the city and of the class warfare that breaks out.

ROCKET LAUNCH
In March, U.S. physicist Robert Goddard (1882–1945) launches the first liquid-fuel propelled rocket near Auburn, Massachusetts. It flies 184 feet.

NATIONAL PARKS INVENTED IN THE STATES
The U.S. Forest Service identifies 55 million acres of American wilderness area in the initiative to preserve regions of natural beauty and geological and ecological importance.

THIAMINE ISOLATED
Thiamine, vitamin B1, is the first vitamin to be isolated in its pure form. This is achieved by American scientist Robert Runnels Williams (1886–1965).

LEFT: The Gothic-style Woolworth Building, at 792 feet high, is one of the distinctive New York skyscrapers. It will soon be dwarfed by even more upwardly reaching buildings.

ABOVE: The Italian airship *Norge* successfully flew over the North Pole this year carrying an international crew.

ZIP UP
Zip fasteners, invented in Chicago in 1891 by Whitcomb L. Judson, redesigned in 1913 by Gideon Sundback and used by the U.S. military from 1914, are being used to fasten jeans.

CHANNEL CROSSING
American Gertrude Ederle is the first woman to swim the English Channel from France to England. She takes 14 hours 31 minutes, knocking two hours off the record.

POWER TO THE WOMEN OF INDIA
Indian women are permitted to run for public office.

MAYAN CIVILIZATION REDISCOVERED
Archaeologists guided by descriptions in books by the nineteenth century American travel writer John L. Stephens rediscover five ancient Mayan cities in the Yucatan, Mexico. They prepare to excavate the largest sites in the cities of Chichen Itzá, Uxmal, and Coba.

BIGGER AND BETTER
Safeway Stores becomes America's largest chain store when Marion B. Skaggs unites the Safeway chain of grocery stores he founded in Maryland in 1923 with a Californian company to create a chain of 466 stores.

FLYING OVER THE NORTH POLE
On May 9, U.S. aviators Richard Byrd and Floyd Bennett are the first to fly over the North Pole. They make the round trip in 15 hours from Spitsbergen, Norway, in a Fokker trimotor aircraft piloted by Bennett, with Byrd as navigator.

A NEW EMPEROR
Hirohito is crowned Emperor of Japan. He became regent for his ailing father, Yoshihito, in 1921. He succeeded him to the throne on his death in December.

HARRY HOUDINI (ERICH WEISS) (1874–1926)

The American escape artist and president of the American Society of Magicians, Harry Houdini, has died. Famous for his ability to withstand any blow, sadly he developed peritonitis after being punched by a member of his audience when unprepared. Houdini, who was born Erich Weiss in Budapest, Hungary, could extricate himself from any form of restraint and frequently escaped from imprisonment in underwater boxes or when suspended in midair. He was a vigorous campaigner against charlatanry.

THE MOVIES SWITCH TO SOUND

Civil war rages in China, but it is also a year of American triumphs: aviator Charles Lindbergh flies the Atlantic solo and sound is introduced to the movies. In the U.S.S.R., Stalin rises to supreme power by exiling, imprisoning, or executing his opponents. Swiss architect Le Corbusier establishes the canons of modern architecture.

ABOVE: A "flapper" with bobbed hair, short skirt, and a new attitude.

OPPOSITE: General Chiang Kai-shek, bracketed by his guards, visits the Ming Tombs at Nanking.

1927

Feb	9	Revolution in Portugal is crushed after heavy fighting
Mar	21	In China, the Nationalists capture Shanghai
May	20–21	U.S. aviator Charles Lindbergh makes the first solo airplane flight across the Atlantic
July	15	In Austria, troops crush a riot in Vienna
Sep	14	Dancer Isadora Duncan dies in an accident at the age of 49
	30	New York Yankee Babe Ruth hits 60 home runs in one season
Oct	6	Premiere of *The Jazz Singer*, first film to contain live dialogue
Nov	3	Lt. General A. Montgomery-Massingberd forecasts war with Germany within twenty years
Dec	19	In China, Nationalists execute 600 alleged Communists

ABOVE: American aviator Charles A. Lindbergh lands safely at Le Bourget near Paris after his pioneering nonstop flight from New York.

ABOVE: The single engine *Spirit of St. Louis*, Lindbergh's record-breaking plane. It was funded by the citizens of St. Louis, Missouri.

STORMY WEATHER
Freezing blizzards in Britain end a year of disastrous weather, devastation, and casualties. Floods hit Britain in February, devastate the Mississippi Valley in May, Galicia, Poland in September, and in November, even Algeria is flooded.

CIVIL WAR IN CHINA
Kuomintang Nationalist forces capture the port of Shanghai from northern warlords and continue their campaigns to unite the country under the leadership of Chiang Kai-shek. The Kuomintang soon remove Communists from the party, leading to increasing tension between the two sides and eventual civil war.

TROUBLE IN VIENNA
Riots and a general strike break out in the Austrian capital after three anti-Socialists were acquitted of the murder of two Communists. Troops loyal to the government crush the strike, but the Austrian government is now seriously weakened.

STALIN TRIUMPHS
Stalin finally wins total control of the Communist Party when he expels Trotsky and Zinoviev from the party. The following year, Trotsky is sent into internal exile near the Chinese frontier, while other opponents are imprisoned.

CLOSER SHAVES
The first commercially successful electric shaver, with a cutting surface that moves back and forth, is patented by Colonel Jacob Schick in the United States.

ABOVE: Manchurian warlord Chang Tso Lin being received at the American headquarters in Tientsin, China. America supports Manchuria in the Chinese civil war.

CBS AND BBC
CBS (Columbia Broadcasting System) is formed in the United States when William S. Paley buys a small radio network. In January, the BBC (British Broadcasting Corporation), founded in 1922 from a consortium of radio manufacturers and now incorporated under royal charter, makes its first broadcasts.

LE CORBUSIER SETS THE STYLE
Villa Les Terrasses, Garches, near Paris, is one of a group of Le Corbusier's great houses. It shows all the features associated with this important modernist architect at this point in his career: white walls, long bands of windows, and a roof terrace. No load-bearing walls create large and open interior spaces.

DEATH COMES FOR THE ARCHBISHOP
American writer Willa Cather (1876–1947) writes very movingly about pioneers and missionaries. She details the difficulties they have in adjusting to their new surroundings and their relationships with the local people. This novel is remarkable because of her insight of both the missionary Roman Catholics and the native Americans.

PEKING MAN
Canadian anthropologist Davidson Black discovers fossilized prehistoric human remains near Beijing, which he names "Peking Man." The remains prove to be an example of *Homo erectus*.

YOU AIN'T HEARD NOTHING YET
The sound era in the movies is inaugurated with *The Jazz Singer*, the first major sound picture, starring the Jewish minstrel singer Al Jolson.

FLESH AND THE DEVIL
Greta Garbo's first Hollywood film is also said to be the best of her silent dramas. She is already creating the air of mystery that surrounds her in her later sound films.

ISADORA DUNCAN
(ANGELA DUNCAN) (1878–1927)

The American-born dancer and choreographer, Isadora Duncan (born Angela), has died in a tragic automobile accident. She was the pioneer of contemporary dance, which incorporates the fluid movements of birds and animals, as well as walking, and classical poses. She founded schools of dance in Berlin, Salzburg, and Vienna. Internationally known, and with an ardent following, she has led an unconventional life. In 1922, she married the young Russian poet Sergei Yesenin, who died by committing suicide in 1925. Shortly before her untimely death, she published her autobiography, *My Life*.

ABOVE: The Utitsky Palace in Leningrad inscribed with the Soviet hammer and sickle.

RIGHT: New York from the air: 300 square miles of the Big Apple taken at one bite.

COUNTING THE WORLD
First international World Population Conference is organized by U.S. feminist Margaret Sanger.

RECORD RUTH
Babe Ruth hits a record 60 home runs in a single season for the New York Yankees. Ruth's achievement and more home runs around the league, due to a livelier ball, rekindle America's enthusiasm for baseball.

UNDERWATER COLOR
In January, *National Geographic Magazine* publishes the first natural color photographs taken beneath the surface of the sea, following months of experiment by ichthyologist W.H. Longley and photographer Charles Martin.

ATLANTIC SOLO FLIGHT
On May 20–21, U.S. aviator Charles A. Lindbergh (1902–1974) makes the first solo nonstop flight across the Atlantic in his plane *Spirit of St. Louis*. He covers 3,590 miles in 33.5 hours.

THE DEVELOPMENT OF THE CAR

LEFT: President William Taft riding in the White Model touring car that formed part of the presidential motor fleet. The steam-powered, seven-seater car was built around 1910 and cost $4,000.

ABOVE: Henry Ford driving his "999" racing car at the Grosse Pointe horse racing track in 1903. Racing with him is Harry Harkness in a Simplex.

Since Henry Ford rolled his Model Ts off the production line in 1908, the car has become part of American life. Early models are driven by steam power, gasoline and even electricity, although gas will eventually be the fuel of choice. Women take up driving enthusiastically and a roadster suits the fast-living flapper style very well.

RIGHT: The Model T is the first car to go into mass production, pouring off the line in his Highland Park factory.
ABOVE: Mr. Ford publicizes the arrival of the fifteen-millionth model.

ABOVE: The first electric car is built between 1917 and 1919. The Detroit Electric coupe is shown recharging its batteries. On a full charge, it could travel over 210 miles on a test run, but 80 miles was an average distance.

LEFT: Amanda Preuss at the wheel of the 1915 Oldsmobile Model 44 eight cylinder roadster. She has driven the car from San Francisco to New York City in 11 days, 5 hours and 45 minutes.

BELOW: The stylish La Salle roadster, which was being produced in 1927.

FIVE YEAR PLANS AND VOTES FOR WOMEN

BritISH women get to vote in the same year that veteran suffragette Emmeline Pankhurst dies. Emperor Hirohito comes to power in Japan. Japan and China go to war. Germany, Britain, France, and 24 other countries sign the Kellogg-Briand Pact to outlaw war. Small pleasures include chewing gum and Scotch tape. Mickey Mouse makes his first appearance. In Australia, the Flying Doctor service takes off.

OPPOSITE: Health and strength: a German swimming pool with wave effects and sunshine.

1928

Jan	10	In Russia, Stalin sends all his political rivals into exile
	11	British novelist Thomas Hardy dies at the age of 87
Feb	11	The Second Winter Olympics open in St. Moritz, Switzerland
Mar	29	In Britain, all women age 21 or over are given the right to vote
May	11	In China, Japanese forces repel a Chinese army which is trying to recapture Jinan, the capital of Shandong province
	15	Australia's Flying Doctor service starts
June	14	British suffragette leader Emmeline Pankhurst dies at age 69
	20	Roald Amundsen dies in a plane crash while going to rescue Umberto Nobile, who had crash-landed in the Arctic

July	12	Nobile and his crew are rescued by an icebreaker
	30	George Eastman demonstrates moving color pictures in the U.S.
Aug	12	The Eighth Olympic Games open in Amsterdam
	27	Twenty three countries, including Germany, sign the Kellogg-Briand Pact for the Renunciation of War
Sep	19	First screening of the animated cartoon film *Steamboat Willie*, featuring Mickey Mouse
Oct	1	In Russia, Stalin begins a Five Year Plan to boost industry
Nov	6	Republican Herbert Hoover is elected President of the United States. Many believe that his opponent, Governor Alfred E. Smith of New York, lost because he was a Roman Catholic

NEW BROOM FOR PORTUGAL

António de Oliveira Salazar (1889–1970) becomes minister of finance, with wide-ranging powers. He soon transforms the Portuguese economy, taking dictatorial powers for himself when he becomes prime minister in July 1932.

CHINA TAKES ON JAPAN

Nationalist forces clash with the Japanese army as they advance towards the old imperial capital of Beijing. Although the Nationalists capture the city in June, uniting China under one leader for the first time since the revolution of 1911, tension grows between China and Japan for control of northern China. The Kuomintang leader, Chiang Kai-shek, is elected president of China in October.

PEACE IN OUR TIME

Twenty three nations, including the United States, France, Germany, and Britain, sign a pact in Paris outlawing war. The pact is the work of the U.S. Secretary of State, Frank Kellogg, and the French Foreign Minister, Aristide Briand.

THE FIRST FIVE YEAR PLAN

The first Five Year Plan begins, designed to transform Russia into a major industrial power. In the countryside, smallholdings are being merged into vast state-owned collective farms, requiring farmers to work in the new factories and towns.

THE NINTH OLYMPIAD

Established stars Paavo Nurmi and Johnny Weissmuller shine again, but there are significant changes at the Ninth Olympiad in Amsterdam, Holland. The rise of a rival organization forces the International Olympic Committee to allow women to compete in track and field events. The ritual of lighting the Olympic flame begins in the new Olympic stadium.

BELOW: Fashions reflect a new freedom for women. These are beach and swimming costumes.

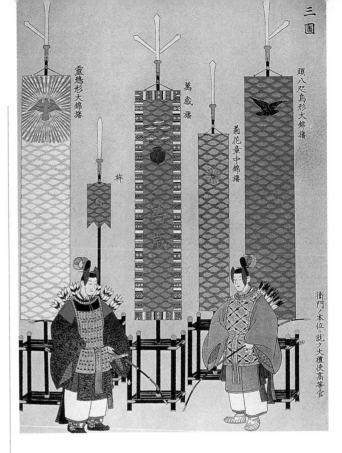

ABOVE: Japanese imperial banners are seen in China, but the struggle between the two countries continues.

CIVIL WAR IN AFGHANISTAN

Amanullah Khan is still trying to introduce reform, but is meeting opposition. He puts his brother on the throne, becomes a rebel himself, and leads a band of guerrillas to depose his brother. Khan's cousin, Nadir Khan, joins in the fight and kills Amanullah. The British support Nadir Khan's claims to the throne. He brings in modern practices, placates the rebels, and restores order. By 1929, the war has ended.

STEAMBOAT WILLIE

Walt Disney introduces Mickey Mouse in this animated film. It is also the first animated film with sound. The mouse is instantly popular, sequels appear, and eventually the character becomes the ubiquitous symbol of Disney. It will become one of the best known logos of the century.

EMMELINE PANKHURST (NEE GOULDEN) (1858–1928)

The English campaigner for women's rights, Emmeline Pankhurst, has died. Married to a barrister and advocate of women's suffrage and women's property rights, she was a vociferous campaigner for the cause. She founded the Women's Franchise League in 1889 and both she and her daughter, Christabel, suffered frequent imprisonment and unfair treatment in the cause. The Representation of the People Act, 1928, passed shortly before her death, was the end of her 40 year campaign and a just and fitting tribute to her.

ROALD ENGELBRECHT GRAVNING AMUNDSEN (1872–1928)

Roald Amundsen, the Norwegian explorer, is missing and feared dead. He disappeared while searching by plane for his fellow explorer Umberto Nobile in the region of the North Pole. During his expeditions in the Arctic, he located the Magnetic North Pole and he was the first man to reach the South Pole in December 1911. In 1927, his book, *My Life as an Explorer*, was published.

ABOVE: Swimming is a major event in the Ninth Olympics in Holland.

THE WELL OF LONELINESS

With its treatment of lesbian relationships, Marguerite Radclyffe Hall's novel creates controversy and is banned in some countries, including Hall's native Britain. Its description of the relationship between a young girl and an older woman causes much scandal. An American court, however, decides that the book should not be banned.

THE THREEPENNY OPERA

Bertolt Brecht and Kurt Weill create a form of musical that admits biting social comment. Weill's music combines memorable tunes and bitter harmonies, while Brecht's words embrace vivid characterization and social satire.

SOLO TO AUSTRALIA

In February, the first solo flight from England to Australia is made by Squadron Leader Bert Hinkler of the RAF. It touches down sixteen times on the 10,981 mile journey.

WOMAN PILOT

In June, American pilot Amelia Earhart becomes the first woman to fly across the Atlantic and is accompanied by two male pilots.

SCOTCH TAPE

The first cellulose adhesive tape is invented by Richard Drew of the 3M Corporation; it is marketed under the brand name of Scotch™ tape.

FLYING DOCTOR SERVICE

On May 15, the first flight of Australia's Flying Doctor Service, founded by Presbyterian minister John Flynn, takes place from Cloncurry, Queensland. The service provides medical help for people living in the remote outback.

PENICILLIN DISCOVERED

Scottish bacteriologist Alexander Fleming (1881–1955) accidentally discovers a mold which produces a substance that kills bacteria. He calls the substance penicillin, but does not study it further.

THE SECOND WINTER OLYMPIAD

The Second Winter Olympics in St. Moritz, Switzerland, sees the return of German athletes banned after the war. Warm weather forces the cancellation of some events and while Norway again leads the medal table, the United States disrupts Nordic dominance by finishing second. Norway's Sonja Henie, though just fifteen, captures figure skating gold and spectators' hearts.

WALK AND CHEW GUM

Fleer's Dubble Bubble gum is marketed in the U.S.

LEAVING AFGHANISTAN

The RAF undertakes the first large-scale civilian evacuation by air: 568 people and 24,194 pounds of baggage are flown from Kabul between December 23, 1928 and February 25, 1929. They are flown in eight Vickers Victoria transports of the RAF's No. 70 Squadron, and a Handley Page Hinadi.

UN CHIEN ANDALOU

The quintessence of Surrealism is reached in this short film by Luis Buñuel and Salvador Dali. At a time when filmmakers are trying to be as realistic as possible, this piece, with its often grotesque imagery, comes as a shock to artists and audiences alike.

BIG BAND VENUE

In New York, The Cotton Club is established. It quickly becomes a favorite venue for the new style of big band jazz, attracting artists such as Duke Ellington and many enthusiastic jazz fans.

FINANCIAL RUIN AS WALL STREET CRASHES

In October, Wall Street crashes and the world trembles. The Pope teams up with Mussolini, and the Graf Zeppelin airship floats around the world in three weeks. The St. Valentine's Day massacre takes place in Chicago. Edwin Hubble proves that the universe is expanding. Foam rubber enters the home and the Academy Awards make their debut.

1929

Jan	**13**	Former U.S. Marshal Wyatt Earp dies in his sleep at age 80
	30	Stalin orders Leon Trotsky to leave the U.S.S.R.
Feb	**1**	Popeye the Sailor Man makes his debut
	11	In Italy, Mussolini and the Pope sign a treaty guaranteeing Vatican sovereignty
	13	Trotsky seeks refuge in Turkey
Aug	**29**	The Graf Zeppelin is the first airship to fly around the world
Sep	**5**	French Prime Minister Aristide Briand proposes a United States of Europe
Oct	**24**	Black Thursday: Wall Street stock market crashes and 13 million shares change hands
	29	Even heavier selling on Wall Street: 16,400,000 shares are sold
Nov	**28–29**	U.S. aviator Richard Byrd makes the first airplane flight over the South Pole

POPE ALLIES WITH IL DUCE

Mussolini signs the Lateran Pact with the Pope, which guarantees the sovereignty of Vatican City. The Pact ends 59 years of tension between the Pope and the Italian state, since the Papal States were annexed by Italy in 1870. In July, Pope Pius X becomes the first pope to leave the Vatican since 1870.

WALL STREET CRASHES

The New York Stock Exchange on Wall Street crashes, with many shares losing up to half their value. The crash brings to an end a decade of rising share prices and prosperity in the United States and sends the economy into a depression.

FLYING OVER THE SOUTH POLE

Richard Byrd, U.S. Naval Commander, makes the first flight over the South Pole as navigator of an aircraft piloted by Bert Balchen. The nineteen hour round trip originates in Little America, the expedition's base on the Ross ice shelf.

HOMOSEXUALITY DECRIMINALIZED

Homosexuality is decriminalized in the Weimar Republic. After lobbying by the Coalition for Reform of the Sexual Crimes Code, the German Reichstag committee approves a penal reform bill removing Clause 175 from the Penal Code, which made homosexuality illegal.

ROUND THE WORLD AIRSHIP

In August, the German dirigible Graf Zeppelin makes the first flight around the world by an airship, starting and finishing at Lakehurst, New Jersey; the journey takes 21 days, 7 hours and 34 minutes.

OPPOSITE: Crowds wait in London's Trafalgar Square for the general election results. Vote numbers and the final result will be affected by newly enfranchised women.

GERMAN PAVILION, BARCELONA EXPOSITION

Ludwig Mies van der Rohe (1886–1969) is the German architect of this structure, one of the simplest of all modernist buildings. The large expanses of glass, simple form, and high quality materials are all typical of his work in Europe and the United States.

VICEROY'S HOUSE, NEW DELHI

In total contrast to the modernist buildings being designed by people like Mies van der Rohe and Le Corbusier, Edwin Lutyens' Viceroy's House is a mixture of traditional styles and elements. Its domes, minarets and details are influenced by the Renaissance.

OPPOSITE: A spectacular eruption from the crater of Mt. Vesuvius: its most powerful outpouring since 1906.

ABOVE: The Middle East is in turmoil. Arabs demonstrate against the Jewish population of Jerusalem, in what is currently Palestine.

THE SOUND AND THE FURY

American writer William Faulkner's novel depicts the decline of the American South through the eyes of a number of different characters, the "idiot" Benjy Compson, the mean Jason, and the sensitive Quentin. This is probably the most ambitious use of different narrative perspectives in fiction to date.

HUBBLE'S LAW

U.S. astronomer Edwin Hubble confirms that the more distant a galaxy is from our own, the faster it is moving away. This discovery, known as Hubble's Law, proves that the universe is expanding.

GEORGES EUGENE BENJAMIN CLEMENCEAU (1841–1929)

The great French statesman, orator, and journalist, Clemenceau, has died at the age of 88. First elected to the National Assembly in 1871, he took a principled stand on many issues, including the famous Dreyfus case (as a Dreyfus supporter). He was Prime Minister of France during the years 1906–1909 and 1917–1920, and presided over the 1919 Paris Peace Conference, which negotiated the Treaty of Versailles at the end of World War I.

SERGEI PAVLOVITCH DIAGHILEV (1872–1929)

The legendary Russian dancer and impresario Sergei (Serge) Diaghilev, director of the Ballets Russes de Diaghilev, has died. Diaghilev first brought Russian dance to Paris in 1908 and established the Ballets Russes there in 1909. Under his direction, the company has attracted the greatest dancers, choreographers, artists and composers of the century. The cast includes the dancer/choreographers Nijinsky and Massine, the artists Matisse and Picasso, and the progressive composers Ravel, Prokofiev, Poulenc, Satie and Stravinsky.

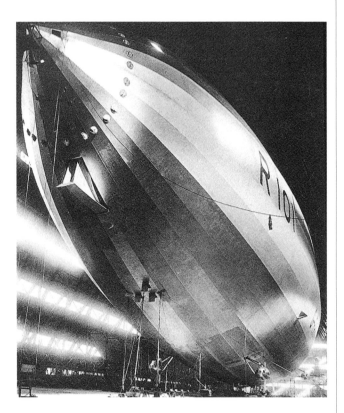

ABOVE: The doomed airship R101 on its test bed.

TROTSKY EXILED

Trotsky goes into exile in Constantinople after being expelled from the U.S.S.R. at the end of January. Many of his supporters are exiled or imprisoned.

ALL QUIET ON THE WESTERN FRONT

German writer Erich Maria Remarque's novel of World War I, seen from the point of view of an ordinary soldier, is an enormous success, and it is said to speak for an entire generation. It shows war in its horrific and non-heroic aspects.

AND THE WINNER IS...

The first Academy Awards ceremony takes place on May 16 at the Roosevelt Hotel in Hollywood, California. It was the idea of filmmaker Louis B. Mayer and it is scheduled to become an annual event.

FIRST IRON LUNG

American engineer Philip Drinker develops the first iron lung, a machine that helps people paralyzed by poliomyelitis to breathe. It will later save many lives.

FOAM RUBBER

Scientists at the Dunlop Rubber Company develop foam rubber, made by whipping air into latex, the white juice of the rubber tree.

ELECTROENCEPHALOGRAPH

German psychiatrist Hans Berger develops the electroencephalograph, a device that measures electrical voltages produced in the brain; a print-out of these voltages is called an electroencephalogram (ECG).

HAIR AND BEAUTY

Colorinse, the first commercial hair colorant for home use, is launched by Nestle in the United States.

ST. VALENTINE'S DAY MASSACRE

Killers dressed as Chicago Police Officers slaughter seven members of George "Bugs" Moran's gang with machine guns. Al Capone is believed to have masterminded the attack.

ALETTA JACOBS (1849–1929)

The Dutch doctor's daughter Aletta Jacobs who, as a result of petitioning the prime minister, became the first woman to study medicine in the Netherlands, has died. After qualifying, she set up in practice with her father, offering free treatment for the poor. A committed feminist, she set up the first birth control clinic in Amsterdam in 1882 and was a vocal spokeswoman for women's health education, women's suffrage, and reform of legislation affecting women.

ABOVE: The German dirigible Graf Zeppelin is sitting on the tarmac
at Los Angeles airport during its three stop transatlantic trip.

WINNERS AND ACHIEVERS OF THE 1920s

ACADEMY AWARDS
BEST ACTOR
1927-28 Emil Jannings *The Way of All Flesh, The Last Command*
1928-29 Warner Baxter *In Old Arizona*
1929-30 George Arliss *Disraeli*

BEST ACTRESS
1927-28 Janet Gaynor *Seventh Heaven, Street Angel, Sunrise*
1928-29 Mary Pickford *Coquette*
1929-30 Norma Shearer *The Divorcee*

BEST DIRECTOR
1927-28 Frank Borzage *Seventh Heaven,*
Lewis Milestone *Two Arabian Knights*
1928-29 Frank Lloyd *The Divine Lady*
1929-30 Lewis Milestone *All Quiet on the Western Front*

BEST PICTURE
1927-28 *Wings*
1928-29 *The Broadway Melody*
1929-30 *All Quiet on the Western Front*

NOBEL PRIZES
PRIZES FOR LITERATURE
1920 Knut Hamsun (Norwegian) for fiction
1921 Anatole France (French) for fiction and essays
1922 Jacinto Benavente (Spanish) for drama
1923 William Butler Yeats (Irish) for poetry
1924 Wladyslaw Reymont (Polish) for fiction
1925 George Bernard Shaw (Irish-born) for drama
1926 Grazia Deledda (Italian) for fiction
1927 Henri Bergson (French) for philosophic writings
1928 Sigrid Undset (Norwegian) for fiction
1929 Thomas Mann (German) for fiction, particularly *Buddenbrooks*

PRIZES FOR PEACE
1920 Leon Bourgeois (French) for contribution as president of the Council of the League of Nations
1921 Karl Hjalmar Branting (Swedish) for promoting social reforms in Sweden and Christian Louis Lange (Norwegian) for contribution as secretary general of the Inter-Parliamentary Union
1922 Fridtjof Nansen (Norwegian) for doing relief work among Russian prisoners of war and in famine areas in Russia
1923-1924 *No awards*
1925 Austin Chamberlain (British) for helping to work out the Locarno Peace Pact, and Charles G. Dawes (American) for originating a plan for payment of German reparations

1926 Aristide Briand (French) for the formation of the Locarno Peace Pact, and Gustav Stresemann (German) for persuading Germany to accept plans for reparations
1927 Ferdinand Buisson (French) for work as president of the League of Human Rights, and Ludwig Quidde (German) for writing on and working for peace
1928 *No award*
1929 Frank Billings Kellogg (American) for negotiating the Kellogg-Briand Peace Pact

PRIZES FOR PHYSICS
1920 Charles Guillaume (French) for discovering nickel-steel alloys with slight expansion, and the alloy invar
1921 Albert Einstein (German) for contributing to mathematical physics and stating the law of the photoelectric effect
1922 Niels Bohr (Danish) for studying the structure of atoms and their radiations
1923 Robert Millikan (American) for measuring the charge on electrons and working on the photoelectric effect
1924 Karl Siegbahn (Swedish) for working with the X-ray spectroscope
1925 James Franck and Gustav Hertz (German) for stating laws on the collision of an electron with an atom
1926 Jean-Baptiste Perrin (French) for studying the discontinuous structure of matter and measuring the sizes of atoms
1927 Arthur Compton (American) for discovering the Compton effect on X-rays reflected from atoms, and Charles Wilson (British) for discovering a method for tracing the paths of ions
1928 Owen Richardson (British) for studying thermionic effect and electrons sent off by hot metals
1929 Louis Victor de Broglie (French) for discovering the wave character of electrons

PRIZES FOR CHEMISTRY
1920 Walther Nerst (German) for discoveries concerning heat changes in chemical reactions
1921 Frederick Soddy (British) for studying radioactive substances and isotopes
1922 Francis Aston (British) for the use of spectography to discover many isotopes and for discovering the whole number rule on the structure and weight of atoms
1923 Fritz Pregl (Austrian) for inventing a method of microanalysing organic substances
1924 *No award*

1925 Richard Zsigmondy (German) for studying colloids
1926 Theodor Svedberg (Swedish) for work on dispersions and colloid chemistry
1927 Heinrich Wieland (German) for studying gall acids
1928 Adolf Windaus (German) for studying sterols and their connection with vitamins
1929 Sir Arthur Harden (British) and Hans August Simon von Euler-Chelpin (German) for research on sugar fermentation and enzymes

PRIZES FOR PHYSIOLOGY OR MEDICINE
1920 August Krogh (Danish) for discovering the system of action of blood capillaries
1921 *No award*
1922 Archibald Hill (British) for the discovery of heat production in the muscles; and Otto Meyerhof (German) for work on lactic acid in the muscles
1923 Sir Frederick Banting (Canadian) and John Macleod (Scottish) for discovering insulin
1924 Willem Einthoven (Dutch) for discovering how electrocardiography works
1925 *No award*
1926 Johannes Fibiger (Danish) for discovering a parasite that causes cancer
1927 Julius Wagner von Jauregg (Austrian) for discovering the fever treatment for paralysis
1928 Charles Nicolle (French) for work on typhus
1929 Christian Eijkman (Dutch) for discovering vitamins that prevent beriberi; and Sir Frederick Hopkins (British) for discovering vitamins that help growth

SITES OF THE OLYMPIC GAMES
1920 SUMMER Antwerp, Belgium
WINTER *Not yet held*
1924 SUMMER Paris, France
WINTER Chamonix, France
1928 SUMMER Amsterdam, The Netherlands
WINTER St. Moritz, Switzerland

U.S. PRESIDENTS
1913-1921 President Woodrow Wilson, *Democrat*
1913-1921 Vice President Thomas R. Marshall
1921-1923 President Warren Gamaliel Harding, *Republican*
1921-1923 Vice President Calvin Coolidge
1923-1929 President Calvin Coolidge, *Republican*
1925-1929 Vice President Charles G. Dawes
1929-1933 President Herbert Clark Hoover, *Republican*
1929-1933 Vice President Charles Curtis

INDIANAPOLIS 500
1920 Gaston Chevrolet
1921 Tommy Milton
1922 Jimmy Murphy
1923 Tommy Milton
1924 Lora Corum
1925 Peter DePaolo
1926 Frank Lockhart
1927 George Souders
1928 Louis Meyer
1929 Ray Keech

KENTUCKY DERBY
1920 Paul Jones
1921 Behave Yourself
1922 Morvich
1923 Zev
1924 Black Gold
1925 Flying Ebony
1926 Bubbling Over
1927 Whiskery
1928 Reigh Count
1929 Clyde Van Dusen

WIMBLEDON CHAMPIONS
1920 MEN Bill Tilden
WOMEN Suzanne Lenglen
1921 MEN Bill Tilden
WOMEN Suzanne Lenglen
1922 MEN Gerald L. Patterson
WOMEN Suzanne Lenglen
1923 MEN Bill Johnson
WOMEN Suzanne Lenglen
1924 MEN Jean Borotra
WOMEN Kathleen McKane
1925 MEN Rene Lacoste
WOMEN Suzanne Lenglen
1926 MEN Jean Borotra
WOMEN Kathleen McKane Godfree
1927 MEN Henri Cochet
WOMEN Helen Wills
1928 MEN Rene Lacoste
WOMEN Helen Wills
1929 MEN Henri Cochet
WOMEN Helen Wills

WORLD SERIES CHAMPIONS
1920 Cleveland Indians defeat Brooklyn Robins
1921 New York Giants defeat New York Yankees
1922 New York Giants defeat New York Yankees
1923 New York Yankees defeat New York Giants
1924 Washington Senators defeat New York Giants
1925 Pittsburgh Pirates defeat Washington Senators
1926 St. Louis Cardinals defeat New York Yankees
1927 New York Yankees defeat Pittsburgh Pirates
1928 New York Yankees defeat St. Louis Cardinals
1929 Philadelphia Athletics defeat Chicago Cubs